creative paper cutting

Creative Paper Cutting

BASIC TECHNIQUES & FRESH DESIGNS
FOR STENCILS, MOBILES, CARDS & MORE

edited by SHUFUNOTOMO

TRUMPETER · Boston & London · 2010

Contents

Introduction

Paper cutting requires nothing more than taking a pair of scissors to a piece of paper and going "snip-snip." You don't even have to draw a design—just fold and cut, and you'll be surprised at what emerges. Don't worry if you fold or cut too much; the results will always be interesting.

This book introduces you to the endless pleasures of paper cutting, from the basic techniques to ideas that you can use in your everyday life.

Paper Cutting Tools

Some paper and a few tools are all you need to enjoy paper cutting. As you create, remember the following points.

SCISSORS

Use a small, thin blade to cut minute details.

X–ACTO KNIFE

If you buy a new knife, look for one with a blade designed for finely detailed work. A #11 blade is recommended.

CUTTING MAT

If you're using an X-Acto knife, you need to protect your work surface with a cutting mat. An 8½" by 11" self-healing mat works well.

RULER

Use a straight edge to draw or cut a straight line. A transparent ruler is especially convenient.

PENCILS

Use pencils to draw patterns, and keep an eraser handy.

STAPLER

Use a stapler to attach a copied pattern to the paper so that it won't slip off while you're cutting.

Paper Cutting Tips

PATTERN TIPS

When you make the items described in this book, start by copying the patterns freehand or photocopying them to the sizes noted. Then use a pencil to trace the pattern on the back of the folded paper. Or you can staple or glue the pattern to the folded paper. Now you're ready to start cutting.

FOLD

1. When using the folds described in Lessons 1 and 2, first fold the paper as directed.

DRAW OR PHOTOCOPY AND LAY OUT

2. Copy the pattern freehand or photocopy it to the desired size, and transfer it to the paper you plan to cut.

CUT

3. Cut along the pattern lines with scissors.

COMPLETION

4. When you have finished cutting, use both hands to unfold the paper.

CUTTING TIPS

Follow these two basic guidelines for cutting:

1. Start with the hard parts and proceed to the simple.
2. Work from the center out to the edge.

Follow these additional tips to make the cutting process easier and your final project neater:

· Use scissors for simple cuts; use an X-Acto knife to cut fine details.
· To make your cuts neater, work with the tip of the scissors and turn the paper as you cut.

· When cutting double fold or thicker patterns, hold the paper firmly with your left hand to keep it from slipping while you cut.
· If you are right-handed, start cutting from the right edge.
· Cut away the excess paper as you work so it doesn't get in your way.
· Keep some of the folds intact on both sides if you want the figures to form a chain.

Lesson 1

THE BASICS OF FOLDING
AND CUTTING PAPER

The first priority is to master the basics of paper cutting, which simply involve folding, cutting, and unfolding paper. Paper cutting uses two types of folds: accordion and layered. The easy-to-follow instructions in this section present a summary of how to make thirty-four different items using the six basic folds; some tips are included to help you design your own creations.

How to Fold Paper ✂

The methods for folding paper fall into two categories: the accordion fold, in which you fold a single sheet of paper in alternating directions, and the layered fold, in which you fold layers of paper into the same shape. These two types of folds are further divided into three categories, depending on the number of folds, for a total of six methods.

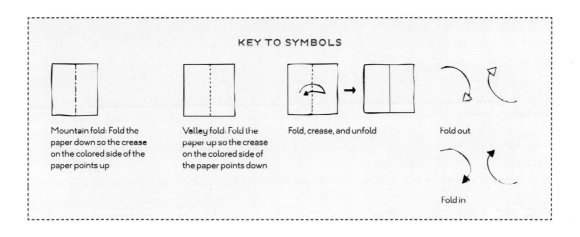

KEY TO SYMBOLS

Mountain fold: Fold the paper down so the crease on the colored side of the paper points up

Valley fold: Fold the paper up so the crease on the colored side of the paper points down

Fold, crease, and unfold

Fold out

Fold in

ACCORDION FOLDS

SINGLE FOLD (PRODUCES TWO IMAGES)

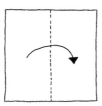

1. Lay the paper down, colored side up, and fold it in half vertically.

2. The finished single accordion fold.

DOUBLE FOLD (PRODUCES FOUR IMAGES)

1. Lay the paper down, colored side up, and fold it in half vertically. Unfold.

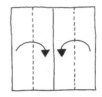

2. Fold each side in half toward the center crease.

3. Reverse the direction of the center fold.

4. The finished double accordion fold.

QUADRUPLE FOLD (PRODUCES EIGHT IMAGES)

1. Lay the paper down, colored side up, and fold it in half vertically.

2. Fold it in half again.

3. Fold it in half a third time, and then unfold it.

4. Redo the folds, alternating mountain and valley folds.

5. The finished quadruple accordion fold.

LAYERED FOLDS

DOUBLE FOLD (PRODUCES FOUR IMAGES)

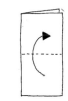

1. Lay the paper down, colored side up, and fold it in half vertically.

2. Fold it in half horizontally.

3. The finished double layered fold.

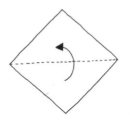

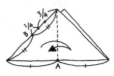

1. Lay the paper down, colored side up, and fold it in half from corner to corner to form a triangle.

2. Crease the center point of the base of the isosceles triangle (A). Make a second crease at a point about three-quarters of the way up the left side (B).

3. Fold the right half of the base up along an imaginary line between A and B.

4. Fold the left half of the base up in the same way to create a triple layered fold.

QUADRUPLE FOLD (PRODUCES EIGHT IMAGES)

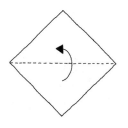

1. Lay the paper down, colored side up, and fold it in half corner to corner to form a triangle.

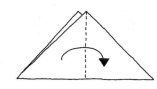

2. Fold it in half again.

3. Fold it in half a third time.

4. The finished quadruple layered fold.

Accordion Fold 01

SINGLE FOLD (INSTRUCTIONS ON PAGE 15)

The single accordion fold is extremely simple because all you have to do is fold the paper once. Use it for designs that display either left-to-right symmetry or top-to-bottom symmetry or for patterns that contain two figures.

HOW TO CUT THE HEART AND BIRDS PATTERN

FOLD

1. Lay a piece of 6"-square paper, colored side up, on your work surface. Fold it in half.

DRAW

2. With the fold of the paper on the left, draw the pattern on the paper or enlarge it with a photocopier and staple or glue it to the folded paper.

CUT

3. Use scissors to cut the bird shape inside the heart.

4. After you finish cutting the inside pattern lines, use scissors to cut the heart shape. Your cuts will be neater if you make small cuts with just the tip of the scissors.

5. Cut the little indentations in the top and bottom of the heart.

COMPLETION

6. When you have finished cutting, unfold the paper to see the result.

Enlarge 250%

Heart and Birds

The heart and birds motif shows why single-fold designs are so attractive. The two birds face each other and appear to be kissing, while the heart shape is symmetrical. The spot where the birds' beaks meet is very narrow, so take care not to cut it accidentally.

SINGLE ACCORDION FOLD PATTERNS

Note: Enlarge the patterns 250%. Use 6"-square paper.

A. MIRROR

A mirror decorated with a ribbon reflects three cosmetics bottles. Use an X-Acto knife for the ribbon cutout, then switch to scissors for the rest of the inner forms.

B. BALLERINAS

The two ballerina figures dancing with hands joined present a charmingly romantic scene. Cut the frame with scissors and the inside pattern with an X-Acto knife. The dancers' hands require careful cutting.

C. MERMAIDS

Cut the hands and legs with scissors, then cut the outline of the bodies. Shifting the position of the paper makes the job easier and the results more attractive. Make the cuts that represent the scales with an X-Acto knife.

D. RABBITS

Cut the outline with scissors. The plant in the middle is finely detailed, so cut carefully. Each time you cut a detailed pattern successfully, your paper cutting skills improve.

A. Mirror

B. Ballerinas

C. Mermaids

D. Rabbits

Accordion Fold 02

DOUBLE FOLD (INSTRUCTIONS ON PAGE 16)

With the double accordion fold, you can cut one picture and unfold the paper to find four. Cut the figures of people or animals, and they'll look as if they're back to back or front to front.

HOW TO CUT THE CANDELABRA PATTERN

FOLD

1. Start with a 6"-square piece of paper. Fold the paper in half using a mountain fold, then fold both sides up into valley folds, as shown above. The result is a piece of paper folded into equal fourths.

DRAW

2. With the folds of the paper on the left and right, draw the pattern on the paper or enlarge it with a photocopier and staple or glue it to the folded paper.

CUT

3. When you cut double fold or thicker patterns, hold the paper firmly with your left hand so it doesn't slip while you are cutting. If you're right-handed, it's easier to start cutting from the right edge.

4. Cut the right side of the candle, then turn the paper 180° to cut the left side. Be sure to use scissors with thin, sharp blades to cut the details.

5. Cut away the excess paper as you work so it doesn't get in your way. For example, after you cut the outline of the candle on the right, discard the paper around it.

COMPLETION

6. When you have finished cutting, unfold the paper to see the result. The right-to-left symmetry of the pattern yields a chain of four identical figures.

[24]

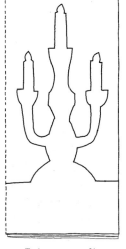

Enlarge 250 %

Candelabra

Your work will proceed smoothly if you turn the paper as you cut to help move the scissors around the outline.

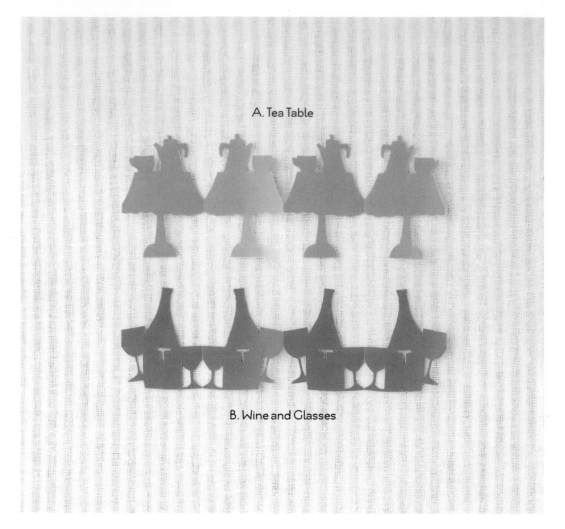

A. Tea Table

B. Wine and Glasses

DOUBLE ACCORDION FOLD PATTERNS

Note: Enlarge the patterns 125%. Use 6"-square paper.

A. TEA TABLE

A teapot and cups sit on top of a table. Be sure that the leg of the table is centered. Cut the pattern lines with scissors, shifting the paper back and forth as you cut.

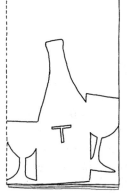

B. WINE AND GLASSES

First, cut the letter "T" out of the bottle with an X-Acto knife. Then use the knife to cut the paper around the stems of the glasses. This work requires very fine cuts and a steady hand to keep the stems intact.

C. Hula Dancers

D. Deer

C. HULA DANCERS

This line of hula dancers evokes a lively luau so well that you can almost hear the dancers' voices. With an X-Acto knife, cut the slashes that represent the leaves in the skirt, then cut the legs, and finally the rest.

D. DEER

Use an X-Acto knife to cut the legs and the antlers. Until you gain some confidence, it's safer to cut broad outlines, then go back to cut the details. Being able to cut patterns like this without much difficulty is the mark of an expert.

✂ Accordion Fold 03

QUADRUPLE FOLD (INSTRUCTIONS ON PAGES 16–17)

A quadruple accordion fold is a double accordion fold carried one step further to produce multiple copies of the same pattern. This technique also multiplies your paper cutting enjoyment. However, the thicker your paper is folded, the tighter you'll have to hold on to it while cutting.

HOW TO CUT THE ROW OF TREES PATTERN

FOLD

1. Start with a 6"-square piece of paper. Fold the paper in half, then make two more folds as shown above. Crease it, making sure that you have alternating mountain and valley folds.

DRAW

2. With the folds of the paper on the left and right, draw the pattern on the paper or enlarge it with a photocopier and staple or glue it to the folded paper.

CUT

3. Quadruple accordion folds are thick, making it easier to cut with an X-Acto knife than with scissors. For efficiency, cut the lines in groups by the direction in which they run.

4. When you have finished cutting all the lines that run in one direction, turn the paper 180° and cut the lines that run in the other direction.

5. Finish cutting and unfold the paper. If you were unable to cut some spots properly due to the thickness of the paper, trim them now with an X-Acto knife, carefully cutting away any excess paper.

COMPLETION

6. Review the final results.

Row of Trees

If you make a pattern with two halves of a different tree, you can make a row of alternating symmetrical trees. With a quadruple accordion fold, you can make more complicated patterns, such as this one, in which two different halves create alternating figures.

Actual size

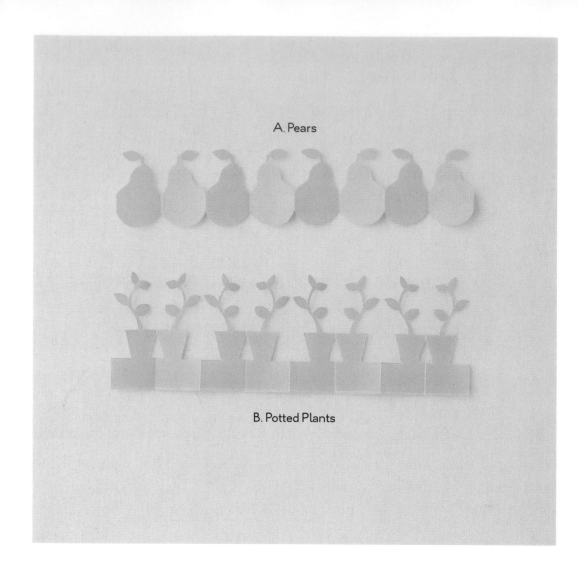

A. Pears

B. Potted Plants

QUADRUPLE ACCORDION FOLD PATTERNS

Note: Patterns shown at actual size. Use 6"-square paper.

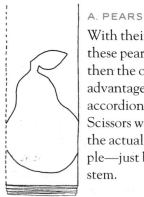

A. PEARS

With their irregular shapes, these pears face first one way, then the other, taking full advantage of the quadruple accordion fold technique. Scissors work well because the actual pattern is simple—just be careful with the stem.

B. POTTED PLANTS

A plant with four leaves is sprouting out of a flowerpot. If you cut this pattern with scissors, start at the tip of each leaf and cut toward the stem before cutting the stem itself. You'll be less likely to make mistakes this way.

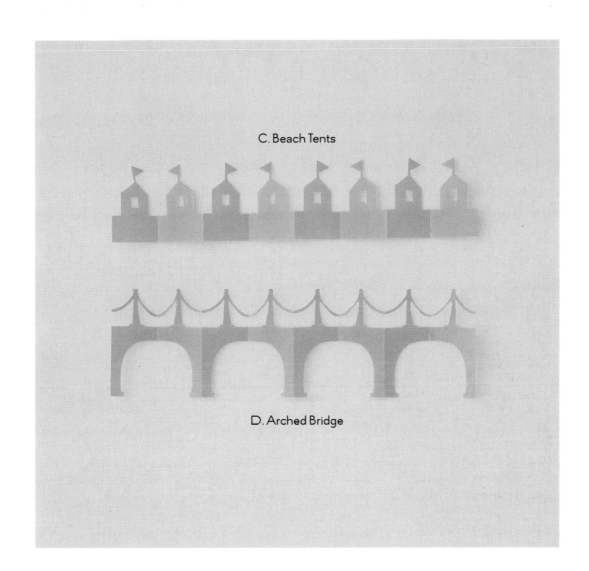

C. Beach Tents

D. Arched Bridge

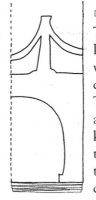

C. BEACH TENTS

This tent with a triangular flag is a simple pattern made up entirely of straight lines, but it's still quite appealing. Start by cutting the square window with an X-Acto knife. Then cut the rest with scissors: first the flag, then the tent.

D. ARCHED BRIDGE

The top of the bridge is left-to-right symmetrical, while the pattern for the arch creates matching halves. The final result is a wonderful arched bridge. Use an X-Acto knife to cut this pattern. Cut the arch first, then the pillars, then the cables. Be sure all the cables are the same thickness.

Layered Fold 01

DOUBLE FOLD (INSTRUCTIONS ON PAGE 17)

If you create a double layered fold from a square sheet of paper, you end up with a pattern in which four identical objects radiate from the center in four directions or form a large circle.

HOW TO CUT THE CROWNS PATTERN

FOLD

1. Start with a 6"-square piece of paper. Fold the paper in half vertically, then fold it in half again to make a square as shown above.

DRAW

2. With the folds of the paper on the left and bottom, draw the pattern on the paper or enlarge it with a photocopier and staple or glue it to the folded paper.

CUT

3. It's easiest to cut from the inside to the outside, so start by cutting the inside of the crowns. Use an X-Acto knife for any parts that are hard to reach with scissors.

4. Alternate between scissors and the knife until you have cut out the middle.

5. Cut the outline of the crowns with scissors. Note: Starting with the most detailed parts allows you to cut the part where you are holding the paper last. This way, the paper won't slip from your hand.

COMPLETION

6. When you have finished cutting, unfold the paper to see the result.

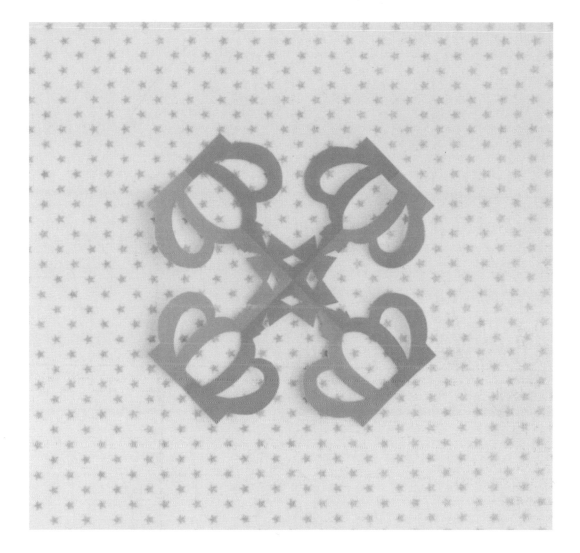

Enlarge 125%

Crowns

Four crowns linked in the middle create a design that looks like a family crest. Cutting two half-crown shapes on a double folded square (on the left and bottom, as shown on the left) yields four crowns.

DOUBLE LAYERED FOLD PATTERNS

Note: Enlarge the pattern 125%. Use 6"-square paper.

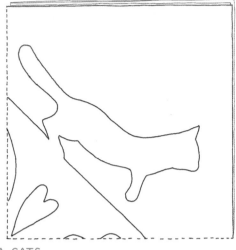

A. CATS

Looking as if they have found some food or heard their owner calling, four cats are rising up on their hind legs. Cut the heart shape with an X-Acto knife and the rest of the pattern with scissors.

B. DANCERS

This pattern is rather difficult to cut due to the large number of fine details. Use scissors and an X-Acto knife to cut the outline of the dancer, then carefully cut the wheel and the leaves with the knife.

C. WILDFLOWERS

Two kinds of flowers spring forth from a grassy plain. Start by cutting the petals with scissors, then the leaves and stems. Turn the paper to make it easier to cut the rest.

D. AIRPLANES

This simple pattern is perfect for beginners. If you cut from the lower left, the patterns will link up. The end result shows four planes that appear to be flying in a circle.

A. Cats

B. Dancers

C. Wildflowers

D. Airplanes

Layered Fold 02

TRIPLE FOLD (INSTRUCTIONS ON PAGE 18)

To create the triple layered fold, you need to fold a triangle at 60° angles, like the napkins in a restaurant. This fold yields surprising results, producing beautiful forms that you wouldn't expect from the patterns.

HOW TO CUT THE SNOWFLAKE 1 PATTERN

FOLD

1. Start with a 6"-square piece of paper. Fold the paper in half corner to corner to form a triangle. Then fold the ends of the base up at a 60° angle so that they overlap, as shown above.

DRAW

2. Lay the paper flat, then draw the pattern on the paper or enlarge it with a photocopier and staple or glue it to the folded paper.

CUT

3. Start cutting the pattern, following the straight lines. To make this pattern easier, cut the excess paper away in small sections.

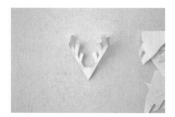

4. Patterns that contain only straight lines are great for beginners. The best and most interesting feature of triple fold patterns is that you can't always predict what the finished project will look like.

COMPLETION

5. When you have finished cutting, unfold the paper to see the result.

Snowflake 1

As a rule, triple layered fold patterns produce designs with six elements. The most typical six-part pattern is the snowflake, and this pattern is the simplest kind. Imagine producing a mysteriously beautiful result simply by cutting straight lines. That's one of the pleasures of paper cutting!

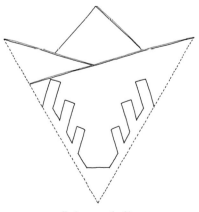

Enlarge 165 %

TRIPLE LAYERED FOLD PATTERNS

Note: Enlarge the patterns 165%. Use 6"-square paper.

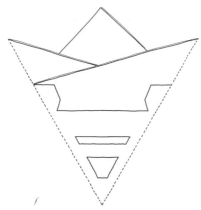

A. SNOWFLAKE 2

This pattern is another beginner's project made up entirely of straight lines. Remember to cut from the inside out. Use an X-Acto knife to cut the middle and scissors to cut the outline.

B. SNOWFLAKE 3

Few people can imagine the result on the opposite page simply by looking at this pattern. Cutting a lot away doesn't leave much space for holding the paper, so be careful this snowflake doesn't slip out of your hand.

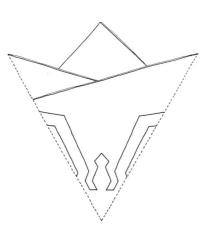

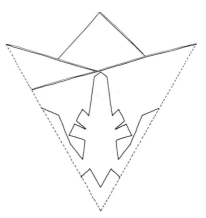

C. SNOWFLAKE 4

Like Snowflake 3, this pattern doesn't leave much paper for you to hold on to, so you may want to staple the pattern in place. Use scissors to cut the middle, then the outline.

D. SNOWFLAKE 5

This snowflake design is particularly beautiful. Given symmetrical patterns like Snowflakes 1 through 5, you can fold the paper in half again and resize the pattern appropriately to produce twelve-part creations.

A. Snowflake 2

B. Snowflake 3

C. Snowflake 4

D. Snowflake 5

MORE TRIPLE LAYERED FOLD PATTERNS

Note: Enlarge the patterns 165%.

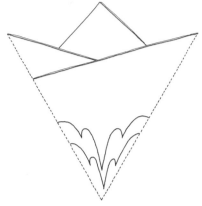

A. SPOONS AND FORKS

Turn one spoon and one fork into twelve utensils. Cut the markings in the handle with an X-Acto knife first; then cut the outlines with scissors. Turn the paper to cut the tines of the fork.

B. PATRINIA BLOSSOM

Cutting from the center of the blossom is too difficult, so start by carefully cutting the graceful curves of the outline with scissors, then cut the inner curves.

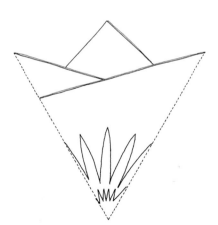

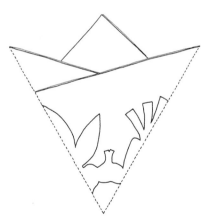

C. DAHLIA BLOSSOM

When you cut the petals, start at the tips and cut toward the center, then cut back toward the outer edge. Even if the petals don't quite match, you'll find cutting with those zigzag motions to be oddly enjoyable.

D. RADISHES AND CARROTS

Cutting the center of the pattern last will make it easier to hold on to, so start with the outline. Keep shifting the paper, and cut the radish leaves by approaching them from both directions.

A. Spoons and Forks

B. Patrinia Blossom

C. Dahlia Blossom

D. Radishes and Carrots

✂ Layered Fold 03

QUADRUPLE FOLD (INSTRUCTIONS ON PAGE 19)

Fold a piece of paper into a triangle three times to form an isosceles triangle, cut, and you'll end up with an eight-sided shape. When you unfold these designs, you'll be thrilled with the unexpected results.

HOW TO CUT THE LACE DOILY PATTERN

FOLD

1. Start with a 6"-square piece of paper. Fold the paper in half corner to corner to form a triangle. Fold that triangle into a second triangle. Then fold it again to form a third isosceles triangle.

DRAW

2. With the long edge on the left, draw the pattern on the paper or enlarge it with a photocopier and staple or glue it to the folded paper.

CUT

3. Follow the two basic principles of cutting: inside to outside, and smaller details to larger outlines. First, cut the middle, oval-shaped pattern lines with an X-Acto knife.

4. Switch to scissors, and cut the remaining openings in the middle of the sheet.

5. Cut the outline of the lace with scissors. Move your hands to create a wave pattern with tiny indentations.

COMPLETION

6. When you have finished cutting, unfold the paper to see the result.

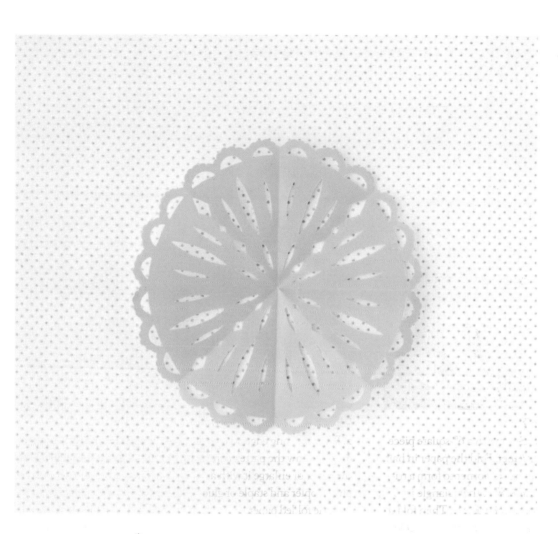

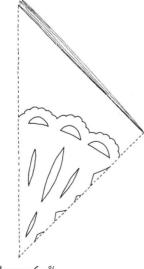

Lace Doily

This pattern, with its many tiny indentations and countless openings in the middle, looks like fine lace. The secret is that each single cut becomes eight cuts.

Enlarge 165%

QUADRUPLE LAYERED FOLD PATTERNS

Note: Enlarge the patterns 125%. Use 6"-square paper.

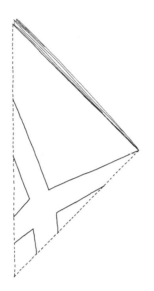

A. STAR

You'll be amazed that this simple pattern cut with scissors can turn into an elaborate star when you unfold it. How lovely to see the little stars inside the larger star.

B. CHANDELIER

This completed pattern looks incredibly difficult, but it's simple and clear enough to cut with scissors. However, the pattern is finely detailed, so be careful to keep all of the parts intact.

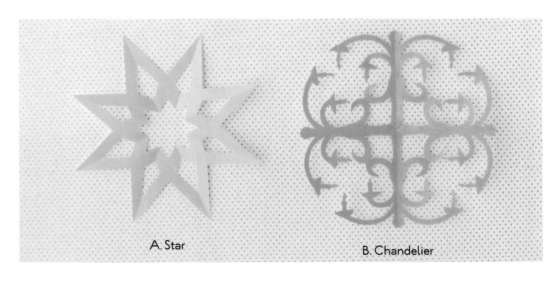

A. Star

B. Chandelier

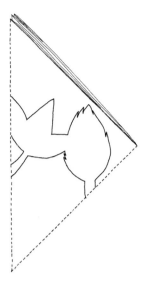

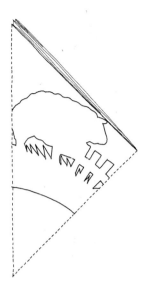

C. LEAVES

To create this stunning wreath, all you have to do is start cutting the outer edges and then the inside edges with scissors. Save the little indentations in the leaves until last, and you're finished.

D SHEEP

First use an X-Acto knife to cut the legs, the blades of grass, and the space between the boards of the fence. Next cut the outline of the sheep and the outside edges of the fence with scissors. Cut the center last.

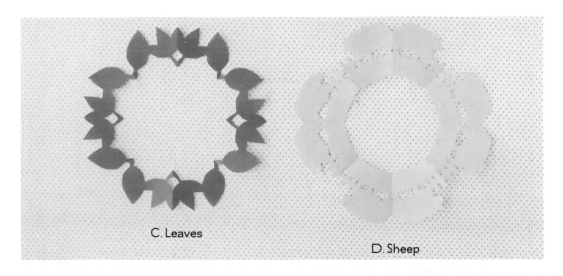

C. Leaves

D. Sheep

Lesson 2

PROJECTS MADE WITH CUT PAPER

You can choose your favorite paper, make beautifully prepared cutouts, and get even more pleasure from your creations by making them into other objects. In this section, you'll find creative ideas for using your paper cutouts. The first six projects show you how to use paper art from Lesson 1. The remaining projects feature some enjoyable ideas for paper art inspired by artist Chinatsu Kohara.

🜂 .... *Project 01* ....

GREETING CARDS FOR ALL OCCASIONS

Take any of the patterns you cut in Lesson 1 and use them to make custom cards in any shape or size.

Happy Birthday

Use the Hula Dancers pattern on page 27.

How are you?

Use the Leaves pattern on page 45.

BIRTHDAY CARD 1

Create a horizontally oriented birthday card based on the Hula Dancers pattern. Aqua-colored dancers on a pale blue background give a particularly graceful impression. (Instructions on page 98.)

GREETING CARD

Fold the circle of leaves cutout in half and glue half on the front and half on the back to make a note card. You can even stamp a message on the front. (Instructions on page 98.)

Use the Heart and Birds pattern on page 21.

Thank you

HAPPY BIRTHDAY

Use the Snowflake 1 pattern on page 37.

THANK YOU CARD

The Heart and Birds pattern is perfect for an everyday thank you card. The added words make the pattern stand out even more. (Instructions on page 98.)

BIRTHDAY CARD 2

This greeting card will bring joy to a friend who has a winter birthday. The blue snowflake, especially when placed on a white card, gives an impression of purity. (Instructions on page 98.)

COLLAGES

You can make collages by taking a single pattern and cutting it in different colors or combining it with different materials. Add numbers and letters to any layout as you wish.

FLOWER COLLAGE

Layer white blossoms on the bottom and pastel blossoms on the top for an eye-catching display. Use double-sided tape to hold the flower patterns in place on a hemp cloth background. Place your finished picture on the floor or hang it on the wall.

Use the Dahlia and Patrinia Blossom patterns on page 40.

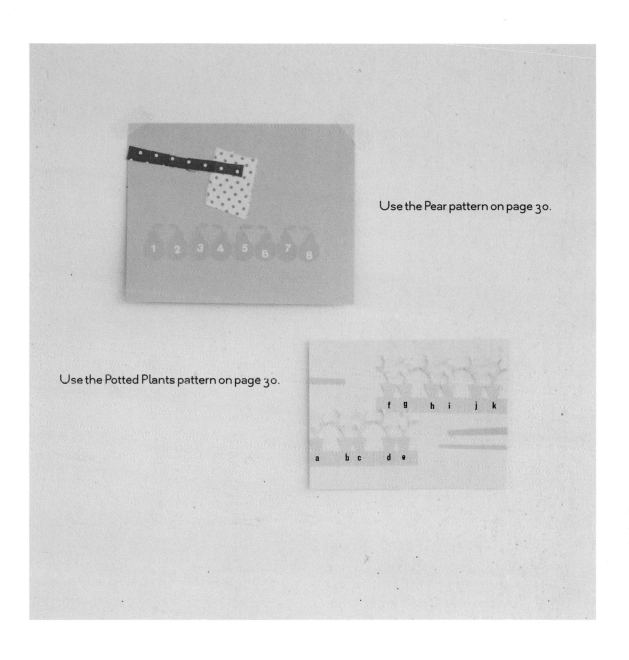

Use the Pear pattern on page 30.

Use the Potted Plants pattern on page 30.

PEARS AND DOTS

Take pear-shaped paper art and two scraps of fabric, arrange them to create a pleasing and balanced layout, and glue them on a background. Use premade letter or number stickers or stamps as accents, or draw numbers or letters by hand.

POTTED PLANTS IN TWO COLORS

Calling to mind plants on a veranda, this pattern features potted plant cutouts in two colors. Apply glue only to the flowerpots so that the leaves and blossoms stand out a bit. Place three strips of paper in the blank spaces, and use letter stickers for additional decoration.

BOOK COVERS

Here's an idea for making distinctive book covers: just add a paper cutout, and you'll have a book cover like no one else's.

Use the Beach Tents pattern on page 31.

Use the Lace Doily pattern on page 43.

BEACH TENTS

Green paper makes a cover for a paperback book. Adding the beach tents cutout gives the whole cover a fresh, airy feel. (Instructions on page 99.)

LACE DOILY

A blue lace doily on a white book cover creates an air of refinement. A lace ribbon makes an ideal accent. (Instructions on page 99.)

CUP AND PENHOLDER

Paper cutting is the perfect alternative for creative people who can't draw. Simply cut out a paper figure and glue it on any object. You'll end up with a decoration that has the same graphic quality as a drawing.

PINK BALLERINA

Glue a single figure of a ballerina on paper cups to create a festive atmosphere for home entertaining, or glue the same figure on a penholder.

Use the Ballerinas pattern on page 22.

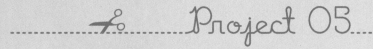

DECORATING A DESK

Take an accordion fold cutout, and set it up on your desk for a casual and charming effect.

DEER AND ROW OF TREES

One quick glance reveals four deer standing in the forest. With a bit of imagination, you can create a whole little world on your desktop.

Use the Deer pattern on page 27 and the Row of Trees pattern on page 29.

WRAPPING

You'll enjoy giving presents or returning borrowed items even more when you've designed the wrapping yourself.

WAXED PAPER BAG

The combination of semitransparent waxed paper and a finely detailed design makes an elegant bag for handkerchiefs, CDs, or other small objects. (Instructions on page 99.)

Use the Chandelier pattern on page 44.

CANDY BAG

Place paper in a plastic bag, and tie both layers together with a length of raffia to form a package for edible goods. This charming design is ideal for wrapping candy or other small items. (Instructions on page 99.)

Use the Rabbits pattern on page 22.

SNOWFLAKE WRAPPING PAPER

Dress up a plain, brown paper bag by adding a snowflake design. Want to keep the contents a surprise? Fold the top over and seal the bag by gluing a strip of cloth over the opening.

Use the Snowflake 5 pattern on page 38.

CATS ON A BOX

Glue a piece of salmon pink paper to a plain white box and then place a cat cutout on top. The colored paper under the cutout will accent the cutaway parts.

Use the Cats pattern on page 34.

Project 07

WINDOW ORNAMENT

Cut some paper art, and glue it on a window. The cutouts are semi-translucent and become part of the view outside your home.

FLOWER WINDOW DECORATIONS

Walking down the streets in Scandinavia, you often see windows decorated with paper art. Chinatsu Koyama says that using light-colored paper is the best way to make enjoyable window ornaments. (Instructions on page 100.)

Project 08

DECORATING WALLS AND WINDOWS

Chinatsu used colorful rolls of paper to create this decoration, which looks like a Hawaiian lei.

HAWAIIAN LEI DECORATION

"I liked the color of the paper that someone had brought me as a souvenir from India," Chinatsu explains, "and it was easy to cut, so I decided to make a chain of hearts. You can drape it around a window or hang it from the ceiling." (Instructions on page 101.)

Project 09

NOTEBOOK COVERS

Cover your ordinary notebooks with cloth or paper, and then give them a further mark of distinction by adding a paper cutout.

PATTERN-ON-PATTERN NOTEBOOK

Choose a solid-color cutout and glue it on paper decorated in a traditional all-over design. "Both all-over patterns and paper cutting are traditional handicrafts," Chinatsu remarks, "so they go unusually well together." (Instructions on page 101.)

LAMPSHADE

This simple geometric cutout pattern stands out on unbleached fabric. The result is a cool, yet elegant two-tone lampshade of the type found in Scandinavia.

EUROPEAN LAMPSHADE

The repeated pattern of thick lines is cut from paper in muted colors and finished in Scandinavian style. When the lamp is lit, the whole atmosphere of the room changes. (Instructions on page 102.)

✂ *Project 11*

HANGING ORNAMENTS

Photocopy your paper art and use it for printmaking. You can then make as many copies of the same pattern as you want.

WOODEN ORNAMENTS

Make your own Christmas ornaments by printing snowflakes on wooden disks. You can also use these festive creations as coasters or mail them to friends as unique greeting cards. (Instructions on pages 104–5.)

Project 12

STATIONERY

Use paper art resembling Indian *sarasa* prints to add a special flair to writing paper and envelopes. The designs almost look as if they have been stamped on the paper.

STATIONERY

This paper art pattern imitates Indian-style woodblock stamps. The yellow ink looks different on paper of different colors, and the result is stationery that could have been—but wasn't—imported. (Instructions on pages 103–4.)

Project 13

T-SHIRT

Take a paper cutout pattern, scan it into your computer, adjust the size and color, and print it on a sheet of iron-on transfer paper. Then transfer the design to your favorite garment.

T-SHIRT

This simple design cut from double folded red paper morphs into an ideal design for a child's T-shirt. The color combination is wonderful, too. (Instructions on pages 106–7.)

Project 14

APRON

Try printing two different continuous patterns on the edge of an apron. By combining paper cutting patterns and iron-on transfers, you can express your creativity on a wide variety of textiles.

APRON WITH CONTINUOUS PATTERNS

Adding continuous border prints to an ordinary linen apron gives it an entirely new character. Wear your special attire in your own kitchen or use it as part of a café server's uniform. (Instructions on page 107.)

Lesson 3

IDEAS FROM SIX DESIGNERS

One of the best things about paper cutting is the potential to turn your favorite photographs, drawings, or symbols into patterns—and cut them without having to fold the paper! In this section, you'll learn methods that will allow you to take whatever paper is on hand and easily create one-of-a-kind projects.

✂ Idea 01

PAPER SILHOUETTES BY YUKO KUWAHARA

Grab a piece of paper—any piece of paper—and a cutting implement. Yuko Kuwahara encourages you to cut your favorite paper into any pattern you like.

HOW TO CUT THE COTTAGE

MATERIALS

Colored drawing paper (Yuko used high-quality yellow paper), 1 sheet of tracing paper, scissors, X-Acto knife, cutting board, pencil, tape, ruler

DRAW

1. Draw the pattern on tracing paper.

2. Place the tracing paper over the drawing paper and tape it in place.

CUT

3. Following the principle of cutting the difficult details first and then moving on to the easy parts, cut the window panes first with an X-Acto knife.

4. When you have finished cutting with the blade, switch to scissors to cut the rest of the pattern. Be sure to hold the tracing paper in place with your hand so it doesn't slip when you cut the design.

COMPLETION

5. When you have finished cutting, remove the tracing paper.

Cottage

"I designed a small cottage of the type that you see in picture books," Yuko says. "I used a lot of straight lines in the pattern to make it easy for beginners."

Enlarge 200%

You can copy photographs or small objects to beautifully patterned paper and turn them into cutouts. Glue your one-of-a-kind paper art on cards, enclose them in letters or albums, or enjoy them in any number of other ways. (Patterns on page 108.)

HORSE

"I copied a photograph of a horse onto tracing paper and cut that horse pattern out of colored paper," Yuko says. She cut the horse on the right from wrapping paper.

GIRL

This pop art–style polka dot paper is actually wrapping paper. The girl with the ponytail was cut in cameo style.

ICE CREAM CONE

"This pattern is based on an ice cream seller's sign that I photographed on a chocolate lovers' tour," Yuko says. You'll find that copying a favorite pattern and making a paper cutting project out of it couldn't be easier.

Cut the outlines of these patterns with scissors, then cut the pattern lines in the center with an X-Acto knife. Put the cutouts up on walls or windows, enclose them in letters, or use them in collages. (Patterns on page 109.)

HOT AIR BALLOONS

This pattern was drawn freehand from a book of embroidery patterns. Carefully cut out the stars and the spaces between the ropes with an X-Acto knife.

BALLOON

Standard procedure calls for cutting the outside with scissors and the inside with an X-Acto knife. In this case, the string is thin, so cut the letters with the knife first, then cut the balloon.

PEACE

Yuko remarks, "The advantage of paper cutting is that as long as you don't get nervous and don't worry too much, you'll end up with something attractive."

CAMPHOR TREE

This pattern is adapted from an embroidery pattern. Having a piece of paper art like this one pop out of a letter is a pleasant surprise.

PAPER FIGURES BY KEIKO TSUJI

You can use the colors and letters from scraps of newspapers, magazines, and wrapping paper to create masterpieces of paper art—using nothing more than scissors.

HOW TO USE A PAPER SHOPPING BAG

MATERIALS

A medium shopping bag labeled with the name of a retail chain, scissors, ultra fine watercolor pen

DRAW

1. Keiko Tsuji doesn't draw patterns, but there's nothing wrong with drawing patterns before you cut, especially if you're a beginner.

CUT

2. Cut the parts of the bag you want to use to sizes that are easy to handle, then start cutting.

3. When you can't cut any more, turn the paper to make it easier. Incorporate the letters into your design if you can.

4. Make use of the letters on both edges of the pattern and incorporate their colors into the design. Cut the shapes of the people with good balance between lines and curves.

COMPLETION

5. It takes Keiko Tsuji only twenty seconds to finish one of these figures, even without a pattern. Her last step is to add eyes and a mouth with a watercolor pen.

Using a Shopping Bag

The paper shopping bags from Japan's Muji Ryohin chain give the impression of finely crafted cloth, and the red lettering looks sober and dignified. Try using the web address lettering on the gusset sides to enhance the figures of three dancing women.

More Figures from Shopping Bags

The sophisticated use of color and the sense of movement in the patterns give this paper art an air of humor and mischief. Despite the sketchily drawn faces, you get a sense of the figures' emotions and personalities. These creations are typical of Keiko's charming paper figures.

Paper Art from Newspaper Scraps

"The warm hues of the printing on color advertisements in newspapers appeal to me," Keiko says. "I made these from the numbers and *hiragana* characters in color advertisements."

Paper Art from a Candy Bar Wrapper

The black and gold color scheme of a candy wrapper lends character to the whimsical nature of the clothing, linked arms, faces, and hats of these figures.

✂ Idea 03

MOBILES BY YOSHIKO MURAYAMA

Held together with thread and swaying lazily in the air, a mobile adds a sense of calm to any room. Cut two colors of drawing paper together, join them with a thread, and hang them up.

HOW TO CUT THE ANGELS IN A HEART PATTERN

MATERIALS

2 pieces of colored drawing paper or cardstock (same size), 1 sheet of tracing paper, scissors, X-Acto knife, pencil, thread, tape, glue, ruler

DRAW

1. This pattern is symmetrical, so use tracing paper to draw the pattern in a size that would fit on a single folded square (see page 15).

2. Turn the tracing paper over and retrace the lines with a pencil to finish the right-to-left symmetrical Angels in a Heart pattern.

3. Lay one sheet of drawing paper on top of the other. Place the redrawn pattern on top and tape it in place.

CUT

4. First cut the inner part of the heart pattern with an X-Acto knife; then use scissors and a blade to cut the outline.

COMPLETION

5. Glue the two faces of the mobile together, and pass a thread through the concave part of the top of the heart. Your heavenly mobile is ready to hang.

Enlarge 200%

Angels in a Heart

This simple mobile makes use of the single fold (square) technique. "I think of it as two angels facing each other and having a conversation," says Yoshiko.

Tea Time Mobile

This mobile features a tea time motif. "I made it in white, chocolate, and coffee colors," Yoshiko says, "because they suggest flavor and warmth. Try hanging it up in your kitchen." (Instructions on page 110.)

Stars and Snowflakes Mobile

This project employs five-sided and six-sided figures made with straight lines and gives an impression of delicacy and purity. All four pieces are made with white paper, so the mobile goes well with either white or colored walls. (Instructions on pages 111–12.)

Country Themes Mobile

The theme of this three-piece mobile is things you might see while walking down a country road in Europe: swans, sheep, and fir trees. The colors are muted but tasteful to reflect the countryside. (Instructions on page 113.)

Bluebird Mobile

Based on Maurice Maeterlinck's story, *The Bluebird,* this piece of paper art overflows with cutouts of birds, dogs, cats, fire, water, and bread, to name a few. The way the middle of the mobile seems to move attracts the viewer's rapt attention. (Instructions on page 114.)

Christmas Tree Mobile

A white Christmas tree bedecked with ornaments sways slowly, a large present at its base. You can almost hear the children laughing with glee. (Instructions on page 115.)

Idea 04

COLLAGES BY MARI KUMADA

Use small paper art elements to create simple collages. You can cut the same pattern in layers, cut away paper to reveal the color of the paper underneath it, attach pieces of cloth, or make a three-dimensional project. Mari Kumada used all of these techniques to make the captivating creations shown here.

HOW TO CUT THE CAFÉ AU LAIT BOWL

MATERIALS

As much paper as you want in a variety of six colors, a magazine, 1 sheet of tracing paper, tape, scissors, a pencil, glue

DRAW

1. Use a pencil to draw a pattern on the tracing paper. Lay the tracing paper on the paper you'd like to cut, and tape it in place. Make small, medium, and large circles; then lay all the colors of paper on top of one another, holding them in place with tape.

CUT

2. Hold the paper firmly in your left hand so it doesn't slip as you cut. Cut the three types of circles with scissors.

3. Next cut the outline of the bowl with scissors. When you have finished cutting, lay out the bowl and the circles.

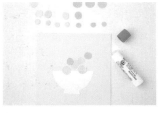

GLUE

4. Glue the pieces in place. Then glue the circles in a pleasing arrangement.

COMPLETION

5. Cut a strip of text out of a magazine, and glue it near the bottom of the bowl.

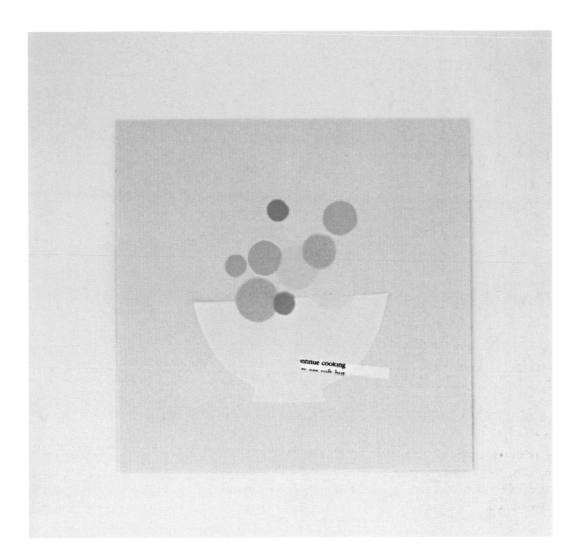

Bowl with Bubbles

"The soft hues and rounded shapes in three
sizes and six colors are arranged to give the
whole work a feeling of movement," Mari
says. The line of text from a magazine added at
the lower right of the bowl is intended to tie the
whole picture together.

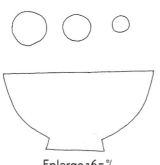

Enlarge 165%

Cat and Cup

A cat peers through the window, wondering if there might be milk in the cup. Cutting out the windowpanes and pasting them to a background that includes the cat gives the entire work a three-dimensional feel. (Instructions on page 116.)

Birds

Three identical birds demonstrate a cutout technique that creates a three-dimensional effect. Make cutouts in the base paper, then place cut paper of the same shape on the base to create the illusion of depth. (Instructions on page 117.)

A Travel Bag

Cut an opening in the picture, place fabric
behind the gaps, and then add the cutaway
paper on top but slightly off center to create an
interesting effect. Affixing the pieces a little bit
off the surface of the base paper gives it a new
sense of solidity. (Instructions on page 118.)

PAPER ART BY HIROMI KOIKE

You can cut paper freehand and make a single picture with carefully thought-out colors and layouts, almost as if you were a painter. Instead of neat, clean lines, you end up with slightly odd but interesting shapes.

HOW TO CUT LITTLE RED RIDING HOOD IN WINTER

MATERIALS

A variety of color paper, hand-made Japanese paper (yellow, white, gray, pink, brown, aqua, red; $4\frac{1}{8}" \times 5\frac{7}{8}"$), scissors, glue, felt pens (nontransparent orange and green)

CUT AND GLUE

1. Hiromi Koike doesn't draw patterns, but beginners will make fewer mistakes if they draw one first. Cut an evening sky out of navy blue paper, and glue it to the base paper.

DRAW

2. Once you decide where Little Red Riding Hood will go, draw her face on the base paper with the orange pen. When the ink is dry, use the green pen to draw her eye.

CUT AND GLUE

3. Cut brown paper for her hair, aqua paper for her skirt, and red paper to make her red hooded cape. Glue them all on the base. Next, cut out her navy blue legs and gloves, place them on the base, and glue them down. Finally, cut the basket and the food.

CUT

4. Place five or six pieces of white paper in layers and cut out three kinds of trees.

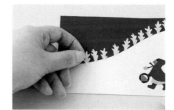

COMPLETION

5. Arrange the trees in random order and at random distances, and glue them down. Finish the picture by cutting out a yellow star and hanging it in the sky.

Little Red Riding Hood in Winter

"This is a pattern I thought up by imagining what the story of Little Red Riding Hood would be like if it took place in the winter," Hiromi says. "Since the pattern is simple, the texture of the papers and the way the trees are lined up give a sense of movement."

Enlarge 200%

Hilltop Observatory

"This scene is based on memories of the scenery near Kushiro on the island of Hokkaido," Hiromi tells us. We see an expansive sky, the road disappearing on the horizon, and the trees, all of which give a sense of perspective. (Instructions on page 119.)

Here Comes the Band!

These musicians march along, playing the drum, saxophone, and guitar. "The uniforms and boots are one unit," Hiromi explains, "so that it's easier to make. All the figures are at slightly different angles, which gives a feeling of movement." Looking at this piece of paper art, you can almost hear the lively music. (Instructions on page 120.)

Setting Out on a Sled

This work represents the Lapland region of Finland. Hiromi says she paid special attention to the angle of the reindeer and sled in order to create a feeling of movement. She drew the folkloric patterns on the driver's outfit with a felt-tip pen. (Instructions on page 121.)

PARTY DECORATIONS BY M&M&M'S

These party decorations and favors made with paper art are suitable for all ages and make everyday life more enjoyable. Cut from patterns and available paper, they allow you to create low-cost but attractive decorations that provide plenty of atmosphere.

HOW TO MAKE INVITATIONS

MATERIALS

Paper (pink, aqua, beige, gray, yellow-green, red), base paper (red and pink; 8½" × 11"), a magazine, paper doily, wrapping paper, ribbon, template, scissors, trimming scissors, glue, pencil, ink pad, alphabet stamps

CUT

1. Fold the two pieces of base paper in half. Trim the pink paper about ³/₈" smaller on three sides. Place the folded and trimmed pink paper inside the red paper.

2. Choose a template, preferably one that features farm animals. Use a pencil to trace the shapes on the paper and the magazine pages. Cut out the shapes with scissors.

3. Cut three narrow strips of paper as long as the width of the card and cut the paper doily in half. Collect the scraps of pink paper cut in Step 1, and choose some wrapping paper.

GLUE

4. As shown in the photograph, take the paper strips, the paper scraps, the paper doily, and the wrapping paper, and glue them on the red paper. Then glue the animals down in a well-balanced, attractive way.

COMPLETION

5. Use alphabet stamps to add "invitation" to the project. Finally, use a ribbon to tie the pink paper to the red paper. Allow the ends of the tied ribbon to hang across the front of the card.

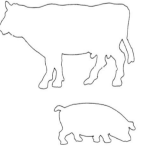

Invitation

Ms. Mitsuma of m&m&m's suggests using a template for paper cutting patterns. "All you have to do is make a few adjustments to the plans," she says, "and pretty soon you'll have a really festive atmosphere."

Enlarge the patterns by 250%.

Crown

This impressive project is made by layering two pieces of paper, making tiny cutouts, and using an arrangement of gold and silver. The result is a three-dimensional work of art. (Instructions on page 124.)

Welcome Sign

Lively letters proclaim "welcome," and repeated ink stamps create the border print. The details are added with pattern-edged craft scissors. (Instructions on page 122.)

Tablecloth

Decorating for an evening of home entertaining can be inexpensive—even slightly
kitschy—but also relaxing. This pattern lets
you enjoy the colors under the tablecloth.
(Instructions on page 123.)

How to Make the Projects

Photographs on pages 48 to 49

BIRTHDAY CARD 1
MATERIALS

1 Hula Dancer cutout (see page 27) or other double accordion fold pattern, 1 sheet of base paper (7" × 8¼")

INSTRUCTIONS

Fold the base paper in half, and glue on the Hula Dancer cutout. Write or print a message above the dancers.

THANK YOU CARD
MATERIALS

1 Heart and Birds cutout (see page 21) or other single accordion fold pattern, 1 sheet of base paper (5" × 6⅞")

INSTRUCTIONS

Fold the base paper in half, center the Heart and Birds cutout across the fold line, and glue it on. Complete the card by writing or stamping a message on the front.

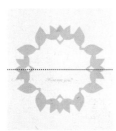

GREETING CARD
MATERIALS

1 Leaves cutout (see page 45) or other quadruple layered fold pattern, 1 sheet of base paper (7⅞" × 5")

INSTRUCTIONS

Fold the base paper in half and glue half of the circle of leaves on the front and half on the back of the card. Complete the card by writing or stamping a message on the front.

BIRTHDAY CARD 2
MATERIALS

1 Snowflake 1 cutout (see page 37) or other triple layered fold pattern, 1 sheet of base paper (4½" × 9")

INSTRUCTIONS

Fold the base paper in half, and glue on the snowflake, as desired. If any part of the cutout spills over the edge of the card, trim it off with scissors. Complete the card by writing or stamping a message on the front.

BOOK COVERS

Photographs on page 52

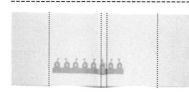

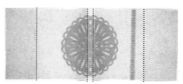

BEACH TENTS

MATERIALS

1 Beach Tents cutout (see page 31) or other quadruple accordion fold pattern, 1 sheet of base paper (the height of the book by the length around the book + 6")

INSTRUCTIONS

Fold the base paper to fit around a paperback book. Position the Beach Tents pattern so it runs across the front, spine, and back of the book near the lower edge. Glue it on, and let it dry thoroughly.

LACE DOILY

MATERIALS

1 Lace Doily cutout (see page 43) or other quadruple layered pattern, 1 sheet of base paper (the height of the book by the length around the book + 6"), lace ribbon 8¼" long, double-sided tape

INSTRUCTIONS

Fold the base paper to fit around a paperback book. Position the Lace Doily pattern so it is centered on the spine of the book, and glue it on. Tape the lace ribbon in a vertical position on the outside surface of the cover.

WRAPPING PAPER

Photographs on page 56

WAXED PAPER BAG

MATERIALS

1 Chandelier cutout (see page 44) or other quadruple fold pattern, 2 waxed paper bags (8¼"× 6⅛" each)

INSTRUCTIONS

Make sure the cutout fits in the waxed paper bag. Place the second bag inside the first, and slide the cutout into the space between the two.

CANDY BAG

MATERIALS

1 Rabbits cutout (see page 22) or other single fold pattern, transparent bag (8⅞" × 4⅛"), magazine excerpt (5⅞" × 8¼"), a string of raffia

INSTRUCTIONS

Fold the magazine excerpt in half, and insert it in the bag. Insert the Rabbits cutout. Tie the opening closed with a string of raffia.

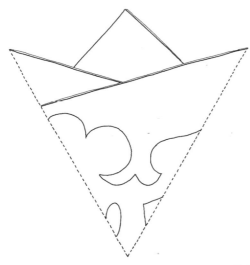 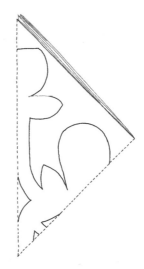

Enlarge 165%

FLOWER 1

MATERIALS

1 sheet of paper

INSTRUCTIONS

Fold the paper to make a triple fold (see page 18), and cut the Spade and Clubs pattern shown above. Cut the inner parts first and then the outline.

FLOWER 2

MATERIALS

1 sheet of paper (cream colored)

INSTRUCTIONS

Fold the paper to make a quadruple fold (see page 19), and cut the Flowers and Grass pattern above. Cut the inner parts first and then the outline.

HAWAIIAN LEI DECORATION

Photograph on page 59

MATERIALS

Rolls of crepe paper for making party streamers
($1\,^3/_8$" wide and any length)

INSTRUCTIONS

Fold the paper in accordion folds (see page 15).
Cut the pattern as shown so the hearts are linked.

PATTERN—ON—PATTERN NOTEBOOK

Photograph on page 60

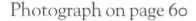

MATERIALS

Handmade Japanese paper ($3\,^3/_4$" × $3\,^1/_8$"), an ordinary notebook, and traditional Japanese paper
with an allover pattern

INSTRUCTIONS

Fold the base paper to fit around a notebook.
Fold the handmade paper following the instructions for the layered double fold (see page 17).
Cut the pattern at right. Turn the paper as you
cut, starting with the outline and then cutting
the inside lines.

Actual size

EUROPEAN LAMPSHADE

Photograph on page 61

Top pattern

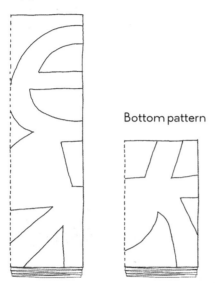

Bottom pattern

Enlarge 165 %

Photograph on page 61

MATERIALS

Handmade Japanese paper for the top cutout (4½" × 18⅞"), handmade Japanese paper for the bottom cutout (2⅛" × 18⅞"), 1 lampshade (7" tall and 18¾" in circumference)

INSTRUCTIONS

Note: If you are using a different size lampshade, measure the circumference of the shade and cut the paper ⅛" longer to allow for overlap.

Fold both paper strips into an eight-fold accordion—twice as many folds as the quadruple accordion fold (see pages 16–17). Do this by folding the paper in half vertically and then folding it four times more in alternating mountain and valley folds.

Trace the Scandinavian-style geometric patterns on the paper. Cut along the lines of the pattern, holding the paper carefully to keep it from slipping. Glue the paper cutouts to the lampshade, overlapping the ends ⅛".

STATIONERY

Photographs on page 63

MATERIALS

Sheets of stationery ($8\frac{1}{8}$" x $4\frac{1}{2}$"), envelopes ($6\frac{1}{4}$" × $4\frac{3}{8}$"), 1 sheet of paper for cutout ($1\frac{1}{2}$" × $5\frac{7}{8}$"), Print Gocco kit (or other printmaking kit)

HOW TO MAKE THE STATIONERY

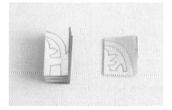

FOLD AND DRAW

1. Fold the paper for the cutout following the instructions for the quadruple accordion fold (see pages 16–17). Draw the pattern as shown on the next page.

CUT

2. Hold the paper tightly, and cut the pattern.

3. When you have finished cutting, unfold the paper to reveal the pattern.

PRINT GOCCO

4. Photocopy the cutout, shrinking the pattern to fit the writing paper, if necessary. Use Print Gocco to burn a screen according to the kit's instructions.

COMPLETION

5. Use the screen to print the pattern on the writing paper. Follow the same procedure for the envelope using the pattern on the next page.

STATIONERY PATTERN

These designs are adapted from Indian wood-block textile prints.

ENVELOPE PATTERN

Like the design for the stationery, the design for the envelope is based on Indian woodblock textile prints. Use paper $2\frac{1}{8}$" × $2\frac{1}{2}$", fold it twice (double layered fold; see page 17), draw the pattern, and cut it out.

Actual size

WOODEN ORNAMENTS

Photographs on page 62

MATERIALS
3 sheets of paper, 3 wooden ornaments 3" in diameter, Print Gocco kit (or other printmaking kit)

INSTRUCTIONS
Fold, draw, and cut each of the patterns on the next page. Photocopy each cutout, shrinking the pattern to match the size of the ornaments, if necessary. Use Print Gocco to burn a screen and print the designs on the wooden ornaments according to the kit's instructions.

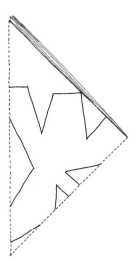

PATTERN (LEFT)
Fold a quadruple layered fold (see page 19), and draw the pattern. Cut it with scissors.

PATTERN (CENTER)
Fold a double layered fold (see page 17), and draw the pattern. Cut the middle with a blade and the outline with scissors.

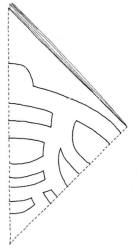

PATTERN (RIGHT)
Fold a quadruple layered fold (see page 19), and draw the pattern. Cut it with scissors.

Enlarge 165%

Photograph page 64

MATERIALS

1 child-size T-shirt, 1 sheet of iron-on transfer paper, 1 sheet of paper for the cutout, computer, scanner, color printer, iron

HOW TO MAKE THE T-SHIRT

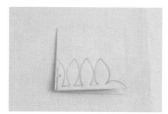

FOLD AND DRAW

1. Fold the paper for the cut-out following the instructions for the double layered fold (see page 17), and draw the pattern shown on the opposite page.

CUT

2. Cut the pattern with scissors.

CUT

3. Unfold the paper to see the results.

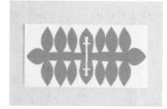

MAKE THE TRANSFER SHEET

4. Scan the paper cutout into a computer, adjust the size and color, and print it onto a sheet of iron-on transfer paper.

TRANSFER

5. Place the design as desired, and iron it on according to the manufacturer's directions.

COMPLETION

6. When the design has cooled, carefully peel off the transfer sheet.

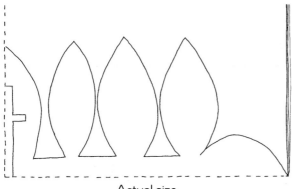

Actual size

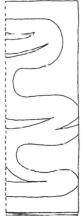

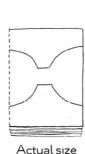

Actual size

APRON WITH CONTINUOUS PATTERNS

Photograph on page 65

MATERIALS
2 sheets of paper for the cutouts (2⅛" × 5⅞" each), an apron
(22" × 23" with ties 28¼"), 2 sheets of iron-on transfer paper,
computer, scanner, color printer, iron

INSTRUCTIONS
Fold, draw, and cut the pattern as shown. Following the instruc-
tions for the T-shirt (page 106), transfer the pattern to the apron.
The pattern will run horizontally across the apron.

TOP PATTERN

Fold the paper for the top cutout to make a quadruple accordion fold (see pages 16–17), draw
the pattern, and cut it with scissors.

BOTTOM PATTERN

Fold the paper for the top cutout to make a quadruple accordion fold (see pages 16–17), draw
the pattern, and cut it with scissors.

HORSE, GIRL, ICE CREAM CONE

Photographs on page 70

MATERIALS

High-quality colored paper, wrapping paper as needed

INSTRUCTIONS

Draw the patterns as shown and cut them with scissors; use an X-Acto knife to cut the more detailed areas.

HORSE

GIRL

ICE CREAM CONE

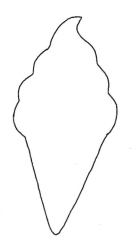

Enlarge 165%

MATERIALS

High-quality colored paper, as needed

INSTRUCTIONS

Draw the patterns as shown. Trim the paper to an easy-to-manage size. Cut the inner letters and symbols with an X-Acto knife, and cut the outlines with scissors.

BALLOON

HOT AIR BALLOON

Enlarge 165%

CAMPHOR TREE

PEACE

SPOON AND FORK

Use an X-Acto knife to make the cutouts in the utensils. Cut the outlines of the spoon and fork and the inside of the circle with scissors.

MATERIALS

2 sheets each of different colored cardstock for the top and bottom patterns (4" square or larger), 2 pieces of colored cardstock for the middle pattern (4¾" square or larger), thread, glue

INSTRUCTIONS

1. Each pattern uses two pieces of paper. Transfer the patterns, and lay them on the two layers of paper.
2. With an X-Acto knife, cut the inner details of the designs and any small indentations in the outline.
3. Cut the outlines of the patterns and the inner circle with scissors.
4. Cut the outer circle with scissors.
5. Pass thread between the two layers of the objects and their respective rings. Glue the layers together. Connect the circles by gluing thread between the layers in the same way.

TEA POT

Use an X-Acto knife to cut the handle. Cut the inner circle and the outline of the tea pot with scissors.

Enlarge 165%

TEA CUP

Use an X-Acto knife to cut the handle. Cut the inner circle and the outline of the tea cup with scissors.

Photograph on page 80

MATERIALS

4 sheets of colored cardstock for the stars (4" square or larger), 4 sheets of colored cardstock for the snowflakes (4¾" square or larger), thread, glue

INSTRUCTIONS

1. Each pattern uses two pieces of paper. Transfer the patterns, and lay them on the two layers of paper.

2. Use an X-Acto knife to cut the inner details of the stars and snowflakes and any small indentations in the outline.

3. Cut the outlines of the stars and snowflakes with scissors.

4. Pass thread between the two layers of each star and snowflake. Glue the layers together.

Enlarge 165%

STAR 1

STAR 2

Enlarge 165%

SNOWFLAKE 1

SNOWFLAKE 2

Photograph on page 81

MATERIALS

6 sheets of colored cardstock (4" square or larger), thread, glue

INSTRUCTIONS

1. Each pattern uses two pieces of paper. Transfer the patterns, and lay them over the two layers of paper.
2. Use an X-Acto knife to cut the inner details of the designs and any small indentations in the outline.
3. Cut the outlines of the patterns and the inner circles with scissors.
4. Cut the outer circles with scissors.
5. Pass thread between the two layers of the objects and their respective rings. Glue the layers together. Connect the circles by gluing thread between the layers in the same way.

SWAN

Cut the opening in the wing with an X-Acto knife. Cut the outline of the swan and the inner and outer circles with scissors.

Enlarge 165%

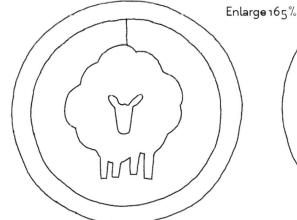

SHEEP

Cut the sheep's face with an X-Acto knife. Cut the outline of the sheep and the inner and outer circles with scissors.

FIR TREES

Use a ruler and an X-Acto knife to cut the outlines of the trees. Cut the inner circle then the outer circle with scissors.

[113]

BLUEBIRD MOBILE

Photograph on page 82

MATERIALS

2 sheets of colored paper cardstock (11" × 6⁷/₈"), thread, glue

INSTRUCTIONS

1. Transfer the pattern, and lay it over the two layers of paper.

2. With the two layers together, cut the small cutouts in the house with an X-Acto knife. Follow the two principles of paper cutting (see page 12).

3. With the layers still together, use the X-Acto knife to make the cutouts in the birdcage, the boy, and the girl. Cut the round and square spaces with scissors.

4. Cut the outlines of the bird, the birdcage, the boy, and the girl.

5. Cut the outline of the house with scissors.

6. Pass thread between the two layers of the bird, birdcage, boy, and girl, and glue the layers together. Connect the figures to the house by gluing thread between the layers in the same way.

Enlarge 175%

CHRISTMAS TREE MOBILE

Photograph on page 83

MATERIALS

2 sheets colored cardstock (9½" × 6⅞"), pieces
of metallic paper as desired, thread, glue

INSTRUCTIONS

1. Transfer the pattern, and lay it over two layers
of paper.
2. With the two layers together, make the candle
cutouts in the tree with an X-Acto knife.
3. Make the cutouts in the doll, snowman, horse,
and presents with the knife. Cut the circles and
the space for the present with scissors.
4. Cut the outlines of the boy, the girl, and all the
ornaments with scissors.
5. Cut the outline of the tree with scissors.
6. Pass thread between the two layers of the
ornaments, present, boy, girl, and tree, and glue
the layers together.

Enlarge 175%

CAT AND CUP

Photograph on page 86

MATERIALS

Paper for the cutouts as needed, a page from a magazine, 1 sheet of base paper (3½" × 6¼"), glue

INSTRUCTIONS

1. Transfer the pattern, and cut each of the elements with an X-Acto knife or scissors.
2. Use the X-Acto knife to cut the windowpanes in the base paper and glue the cat and the background behind the window so the cat appears to be peeking in.
3. Arrange the cup, spoon, and sugar cube (cutting the sugar cube from a magazine page) as desired, and glue them on the background.

WINDOW
(WRONG SIDE)

WINDOW
(RIGHT SIDE)

Cut only the cat's head and torso, and cut the paper for the background slightly larger than the window. Turn the base paper over, and glue the cat into a position where it appears to be peering in through the window. Then glue the background on top of the cat.

Enlarge 125%

BIRDS

Photograph on page 86

INSTRUCTIONS

1. Transfer the patterns, and cut two of the birds with scissors.

2. Cut one bird in the base paper with an X-Acto knife. Turn over the base paper, and glue a different colored paper over the cutout.

3. Determine the position of the other two birds, possibly overlapping, and glue them to the base paper.

MATERIALS

Paper for the birds as needed, 2 sheets of base paper (5⅞" x 5⅞" each), glue

Bird pattern

A

A

A

Enlarge 125%

A TRAVEL BAG

Photograph on page 87

MATERIALS

1 sheet of colored paper, 1 piece of fabric ($7^7/_8$" × $7^7/_8$"), 1 sheet of base paper ($8^1/_4$" × $11^7/_8$"), cardboard as needed (to create a three-dimensional effect)

INSTRUCTIONS

1. Transfer the pattern to the base paper, and cut the woman's figure with an X-Acto knife. Put the figure aside for later use.
2. Turn the base paper over, and glue fabric over the cutout.
3. Use scissors to cut four bare trees as shown in the pattern. Arrange them on the front of the base paper, and glue down the trunks only, not the branches. Fold the branches up slightly to create a three-dimensional effect.
4. Glue together two tiny pieces of cardboard, about $1/_8$" square. Make two more.
5. Glue the cardboard layers to the back of the woman's chest, bag, and right leg. Place the figure of the woman over the hole in the base paper, but shift it slightly to the right. Glue it in place to complete the project.

In the original, the underlying fabric had polka dots. You could finish without placing the cutout of the woman over the fabric.

Enlarge 200%

HILLTOP OBSERVATORY

Photograph on page 90

MATERIALS

Colored and handmade paper as needed, 1 sheet of base paper ($4\frac{7}{8}'' \times 5\frac{7}{8}''$), felt-tip pen, watercolor pen, glue

INSTRUCTIONS

1. Cut the ground with scissors, positioning the road a bit left of center, and glue it to the base paper.

2. Cut the observatory with scissors and glue it to the base paper. Glue the roof onto the observatory, make windows with contrasting colored paper, and add other details with a watercolor pen.

3. Fold the paper for the trees, and make four kinds of trees. Place them at irregular intervals in the scene.

4. Cut four stars of different lengths and thicknesses and place them in different places in the picture.

5. Draw constellations in the sky with the gold felt-tip pen.

Actual size

HERE COMES THE BAND!

Photograph on page 91

MATERIALS

Colored and handmade paper as needed, base paper (4¼" × 5½"), felt-tip pens, watercolor pen, glue

INSTRUCTIONS

1. Hiromi Koike always cuts freehand, but as a beginner, you may find it easier to transfer the pattern and cut the pieces with scissors.
2. Glue the ground to the base paper. Determine where you want the girls' faces to be and draw them on the base paper with a felt-tip pen.

3. Glue the hair and hats to each head, then glue on the uniforms.
4. Glue the instruments and arms to each figure in a way that suggests motion. Lift the hems of the uniforms a bit and glue on the legs and boots.
5. For a bit of extra whimsy, glue musical notes into the background.
6. Finally, use a felt-tip pen to draw the buttons, bootlaces, and eyes. Add details to the musical instruments with the watercolor pen to finish the project.

Actual size

MATERIALS

Colored and handmade paper as needed, felt-tip pens, glue

INSTRUCTIONS

1. Cut the pattern freehand, or transfer the pattern pieces and cut them out.
2. Glue the ground to the base paper. Determine where you want the sled driver's face to be, and draw it on the base paper with a felt-tip pen.
3. Use the face as a guide to gluing on the hat, clothing, hands, and legs. Use handmade paper for the stripes on the hat and clothing; use felt tip pens to create designs on the clothing and draw the eyes.
4. Lift the hem of the garment a bit to insert the seat part of the sled.
5. Glue the reindeer to the base paper, and draw reins with a felt-tip pen. Use a felt-tip pen to add eyes, a mouth, and hooves.
6. Glue the house on the base paper in the lower right corner.
7. Glue a full moon in the upper right corner, and complete the project by gluing the letters for *Hyvää huomenta* ("Good morning" in Finnish) to the picture.

Actual size

WELCOME SIGN

Photograph on page 94

MATERIALS

Paper for the frame and letters as needed, 1 sheet of background paper (11⁵/₈" × 8¼"), 1 sheet of thick paper for the base (11⁵/₈" × 8¼"), 3 types of lace paper doilies, glue, stamps and ink pad, pattern-edged craft scissors

INSTRUCTIONS

1. Glue pieces of lace paper in well-balanced spots all over the background paper.
2. Cut four strips of paper 1⁵/₈" wide, and scallop the long edges with patterned-edged craft scissors to create a frame.

3. Stamp a continuous pattern on the frame paper, and glue the strip around the background paper to complete the frame.
4. Cut out the letters for "WELCOME." Some letters can be simply drawn on the paper.
5. Stamp the poster in five random spots, and glue it to a thick paper backing.

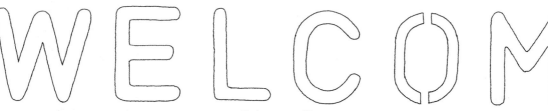

Enlarge 125%

TABLECLOTH

Photograph on page 95

MATERIALS

2 pieces of vinyl sheeting in contrasting colors (35½" × 35½" each)

INSTRUCTIONS

Fold one of the vinyl sheets into a triple layered fold (see page 18) and then fold it in half vertically twice to produce twenty-four folds. Cut the pattern as shown with scissors, and unfold it to see the results. Lay the other piece of vinyl sheeting under the cutout for contrast.

1. To make a triple layered fold, first fold the sheeting in half and then fold the sheet into a triangle.

2. Starting from the left, fold the corner up to form a 60° angle.

3. Fold the right corner up to form a 60° angle and to create a triple napkin fold.

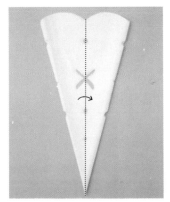

4. Fold in half again to produce twelve sections.

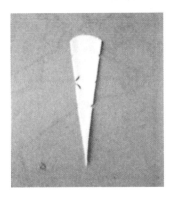

5. Another fold makes twenty-four sections. Transfer the pattern, and cut it out with scissors.

The fold is demonstrated on a finished tablecloth.

CROWN

Photograph on page 94

MATERIALS

Colored paper as needed, lace paper doilies as needed, metallic paper for the base ($7^7/_8$" × $23^5/_8$"), glue

INSTRUCTIONS

1. Fold the base paper in half to create a single fold accordion (see page 15), and transfer patterns A and B.
2. Use an X-Acto knife to make the cutouts in pattern A, and use scissors to cut the outline.
3. Cut pattern B with scissors.
4. Glue pattern B to pattern A, lining up the bottom edges.
5. Cut circles between $5/_8$" and $7/_8$" in diameter from the colored paper and the leftover metallic paper.
6. Glue the circles at intervals around the crown, and glue bits of lace paper on the peaks of the crown.

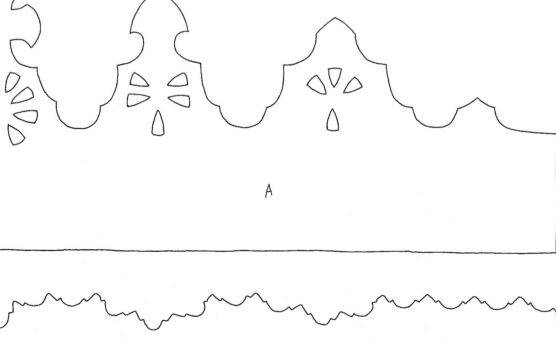

A

B

Enlarge 200%

RESOURCES

CREATIVE PAPERS
http://handmade-paper.us

DICK BLICK ART MATERIALS
www.dickblick.com

HIROMI PAPER INTERNATIONAL
www.hiromipaper.com

KATE'S PAPERIE
www.katespaperie.com

NEW YORK CENTRAL ART SUPPLY
www.nycentralart.com

PAPER ARTS
www.PaperArts.com

PAPER SOURCE
www.paper-source.com

THE PAPER STUDIO
www.paperstudio.com

PEARL PAINT
www.pearlpaint.com

UTRECHT
www.utrechtart.com

CONTRIBUTORS

These seven artists contributed material to this book. Their thoughts and profiles will give you an idea of what is special about each of their creations.

MARI KUMADA

Craft writer and illustrator. She can't resist turning attractive paper into wrapping paper, stamps, bookmarks, or other everyday objects.

PROJECTS: PAGES 20–45, 48–57, 84–87

"I like the fact that you don't need a pattern and can just cut and create whatever you want. Even though it's simple, it offers a wide range of expression, depending on the materials and subjects you choose, and that's what attracts me to it."

CHINATSU KOYAMA

This popular artist and author works in wool, yarn, leather, metal, and other familiar and plain materials.

PROJECTS: PAGES 58–65

"I like the simplicity and strength of the art that emerges from paper cutting. I bring my favorite themes to life in a variety of media. Repeating patterns are fun because they remind me of textiles."

YUKO KUWAHARA

A graduate of Kyoto College of Art (now Kyoto University of Art and Design), she became an assistant there before going freelance in 2003. She designs layouts for fashion, cooking, and miscellaneous merchandise. She also designs handwork projects for magazines.

PROJECTS: PAGES 68–71

"I enjoy getting all caught up in making freehand paper art on favorite themes using favorite materials. I also like the way that attractive, flexible objects emerge from my efforts."

KEIKO TSUJI

A graduate of Bunka Gakuin University and an author and illustrator specializing in paper cutting, Keiko has participated in both solo and group exhibitions since 1998. She works in a wide range of areas, including book cover and graphic design, picture books, and creation of miscellaneous art objects. www.tsujikeiko.com.

PROJECTS: PAGES 72–77

"I feel as if I'm taking ordinary materials that you see every day, such as newspapers and wrapping paper, and finding the people hidden in them. It's fun to see what unexpected shapes emerge."

YOSHIKO MURAYAMA

This author and illustrator has been cutting paper since childhood and has participated in Design Festa, individual exhibitions, and group exhibitions. She also gives paper cutting lessons to children, both in schools and privately. http://kageegai445banti.at.webry.info/ and www.geocities.jp/wandervogel67/.

PROJECTS: PAGES 78–83

"I met Kazuko Tajiri at Design Festa in Tokyo, and that's when I started making mobiles. What I like about [Scandinavian]-style mobiles is their slow but elegant movement and their high-quality use of color."

HIROMI KOIKE

A graduate of Kansai University, she studied at Setsu Mode Seminar before her first group exhibition in 2002. She currently shows her works and postcards at Ceramics Salon Yamamoto in Tokyo.

PROJECTS: PAGES 88–91

"Since I cut without using patterns, I can never make exactly the same piece twice. I just snip away, thinking about what colors I want to use. I love all of it, even the pieces that are misshapen or the ones that I've cut too much from."

M&M&M'S

This four-person, three-studio artists' cooperative is made up of display designer and artist Tomoko Mitsuma, accessory designer "min" (Noriko Misumi), and macarero (Sawako and Saori). They put up exhibitions that include creation of spaces. www008.upp.so-net.ne.jp/m-m-m.

PROJECTS: PAGES 92–95

"We can make sophisticated paper art using templates and our favorite paper. We love cutting paper to produce objects that make life more enjoyable."

TRUMPETER BOOKS
An imprint of Shambhala Publications, Inc.
Horticultural Hall
300 Massachusetts Avenue
Boston, Massachusetts 02115
www.shambhala.com

9 8 7 6 5 4 3 2 1

First English Edition
Printed in China

♾This edition is printed on acid-free paper that meets
the American National Standards Institute z39.48 Standard.

♻Shambhala Publications makes every effort to print on recycled paper.
For more information please visit www.shambhala.com.

Distributed in the United States by Random House, Inc.,
and in Canada by Random House of Canada Ltd

Designed by Daniel Urban-Brown

Library of Congress Cataloging-in-Publication Data
Kawaii kirigami ressun. English.
Creative paper cutting: basic techniques and fresh designs for stencils, mobiles, cards, and more / edited by Shufunotomo.—1st English ed.
p.   cm.
ISBN 978-1-59030-731-1 (pbk.: alk. paper) 1. Paper work.
2. Cut-out craft. I. Shufu no Tomosha. II. Title.
TT870.K32513 2010
745.54—dc22
2010014942